The Morning

Written in Manor Park, u   uss

DANIEL LEHAN

wisdom's bottom press

Published 2016
by Wisdom's Bottom Press

Wisdom's Bottom Press
15 King's Road, St Leonards-on-Sea, TN37 6EA

e-mail: wisdoms.bottom@zoho.com
www: http://www.wisdomsbottom.com/

ISBN   978-0-9935502-2-5

Printed and bound by imprintdigital.com, Upton Pyne, Exeter

to those who come second, third, or fourth

Gallery Play

Cast   Person 1

            Person 2

            (one of whom wears a hat)

Act One   **Gallery 7**

Person 1   He's done really well with the daffodils. Look at the light falling across the petals.

Person 2   Very well indeed.   But he hasn't got the handle at all.

Person 1   You're right he hasn't. But just look at his use of all that thick paint.   It's really hard to squeeze that amount of paint from a tube. Try it.

Person 2   I will.

Act Two   **Gallery 15**

Person 1   He's got the figure very well.

Person 2   It's not quite in the centre.

Person 1   He died when he was ninety-two.

Act Three   **Gallery 22**

Person 1   That frame is nice.

Person 2   Yes, but it's a bit heavy.

Person 1   Like an ornamental rug ?

Person 2   Yes. Like an ornamental rug.

Difference of Opinion

its a dog its a bear its a dog its a bear its a dog its a bear its a dog its a bear
its a dog its a bear its a dog its a bear its a dog its a bear its a dog its a bear
its a dog its a bear its a dog its a bear its a dog its a bear its a dog its a bear
its a dog its a bear its a dog its a bear its a dog its a bear its a dog its a bear
its a dog its a bear its a dog its a bear its a dog its a bear its a dog its a bear
its a dog its a bear its a dog its a bear its a dog its a bear its a dog its a bear
its a dog its a bear its a dog its a bear its a dog its a bear its a dog its a bear
its a dog its a bear its a dog its a bear its a dog its a bear its a dog its a bear
its a dog its a bear its a dog its a bear its a dog its a bear its a dog its a bear
its a dog its a bear its a dog its a bear its a dog its a bear its a dog its a bear
its a dog its a bear its a dog its a bear its a dog its a bear its a dog its a bear
its a dog its a bear its a dog its a bear its a dog its a bear its a dog its a bear
its a dog its a bear its a dog its a bear its a dog its a bear its a dog its a bear
its a dog its a bear its a dog its a bear its a dog its a bear its a dog its a bear
its a dog its a bear its a dog its a bear its a dog its a bear its a dog its a bear
its a dog its a bear its a dog its a bear its a dog its a bear its a dog its a bear
its a dog its a bear its a dog its a bear its a dog its a bear its a dog its a bear
its a dog its a bear its a dog its a bear its a dog its a bear its a dog its a bear
its a dog its a bear its a dog its a bear its a dog its a bear its a dog its a bear
its a dog its a bear its a dog its a bear its a dog its a bear its a dog its a bear
its a dog its a bear its a dog its a bear its a dog its a bear its a dog its a bear
its a dog its a bear its a dog its a bear its a dog its a bear its a dog its a bear
its a dog its a bear its a dog its a bear its a dog its a bear its a dog its a bear
its a dog its a bear its a dog its a bear its a dog its a bear its a dog its a bear
its a dog its a bear its a dog its a bear its a dog its a bear its a dog its a bear
its a dog its a bear its a dog its a bear its a dog its a bear its a dog its a bear
its a dog its a bear its a dog its a bear its a dog its a bear its a dog its a bear
its a dog its a bear its a dog its a bear its a dog its a bear its a dog its a bear
its a dog its a bear its a dog its a bear its a dog its a bear its a dog its a bear
its a dog

Scene Setter

A little to the left.
Are you sure ?
Yes, don't you remember ? You are usually closer to the forest
and behind, slightly right, of the church. So the light catches your
peak and casts your purple shadow on the fields below.
Like this ?
A tad more left . . . bit more . . . perfect ! Now, horses you need to
gallop about a bit. Make sure you stay over by the river so it
catches your reflections. It's a simple trick but one that people
expect nowadays. Trees, you sway gently and make those lovely
rustling sounds. Birds. Sun. Ready ? After ten.
Ten
Nine
Eight
Seven
Six
Five
Four
Three . . .
Hang on !
It's Autumn. Let's start with The Rolling Mist.

Saturday Night Out

Slumped over immense flanks stained with vomit coins from his pocket rattle on cobbled streets clipped by cantering hooves. His helmet - who knows where. Kerbs. Parking meters. Streetlights. The entire town he knows by hand a series of blurs. There's the doorway he moves people away from. There's the shop that sells dodgy goods. And that's the place he confronted the baying baiting jeering mob a few hours before. Erect. Commanding in the saddle. Buttons and stirrups super shiny. Helmet on perfectly straight. Bleary eyed he clings on now for all he is worth. Swigs from the whisky bottle. Snatches a bite of his kebab. Prays that Annabelle knows her way home. Tail swishing his flushed face. Immense. Freeze-framed. Slow motioned by open mouthed colleagues. Back at The Yard.

Unravelled

Oh the countless hours she had spent !
All those intricate stitches he now teases apart.
Wound the wool back into balls.
Purl
Cable
Basket
Moss
Waffle
Chevron
Twin
Windmill

Night Shifts

The insomniac cleaner works at night. Sweeps floors. Polishes
furniture. Stretches to the farthest corner of the bedroom. Dusts
cobwebs. Husband asleep. Below.

The insomniac mathematician counts the hairs on his head.
Calculates the number of breaths he has ever taken. Estimates
those remaining.

The insomniac walker paces her room. Back and forth. The
distance to. The distance from. Saturn.

Documentary

There was always one. Most often a gazelle. Who forgot The Rules.

1   Act natural.

2   Carry on eating, sleeping, having sex, as if they weren't there.

3   DONT ！ DONT ！ DONT ！ DONT ！ DONT ！ stare into the camera.

Good As New

He amassed a collection of ears. Kept on cotton lined trays in labelled drawers. Over time. News spread. People would send those they found with a note. Spotted this on the back seat of the number 38. This was floating in the local swimming pool and naturally I thought of you. Chanced upon this after a recent church service. Would you like it for your collection ? After a brush they looked good as new. Someone handed him a small package telling him. Lost the other so am giving this to you. Then disappeared. Before he could check. If they were pulling his leg.

Personal Information (1)

Now that we are acquainted there is something I feel you should know. It takes 10 minutes 42 seconds to fill my bath. Both taps turned. Full on.

Personal Information (2)

I do not own a pair of clown shoes. I do not have a boa constrictor or pet tarantula. I have no collection of DVDs titled The History of the Tank. I am sorry. I am not. Who you thought. I was.

The Way It Was

Before the invention of walls. Floors and ceilings were separated by Upholders. These Upholders those with strong arms. Firm Legs. Straight backs. The strongest and healthiest. Were highly prized. Hired by the thousand. Palaces. Courts of law. Places of worship. Bearing the weight of chandeliers. Carved stone. Furniture. People. Required that many. Those unable to afford an Upholder held their own floor and ceiling apart. Those living alone fared worse. Should they go out. To work. Pray. Shop. Visit friends. Their room would collapse.

Retirement Village

See the house over there ?
Yes.
Dr Frankenstein lives there. His monster is often seen picking fruit from the trees.
Count Dracula resides in the bungalow behind. The one with the curtains drawn.
And the elderly people queuing outside the Post Office ?
Vampires. Zombies. Witches. Hooded slashers. It's Tuesday. Pension Day.

Left

She was left in shops by her father. Who smiling said. I have to
pop along the road. Will only be a minute. I'll leave her here. She
won't be any trouble. Hours went by and he'd return with tales of
his delay. He'd met an old friend. They hadn't seen each other for
so long. Had started chatting. About the old times. You know
how it is. You'd think she'd grow up feeling bitter. Not a word of it.
Knew how to measure curtains. How to change tyres. To weigh a
perfect pound of potatoes by eye. To lay out the dead.

Sable

Who will buy her ? No matter. As long as she is dabbed in luscious turpentine. Her hairs caressed and soaked in warm soapy water at the end of the day. Left to dry upright. Overnight.

Who will buy her ? Student ? Master ? Sunday Painter ? Given the choice. A painter of landscapes would be nice. But anyone really. Anyone at all. Except a pointillist. No. Not a pointillist. Not a bloody pointillist.

Local Hero

Citizens gathered last night to honour Dr Ryan Walton. Who last month confronted a bear mauling a patient in his waiting room. The beast fled. Back across the ice. Into the woods. After calling an ambulance Dr Walton resumed his work fitting a Maryland Bonded Bridge. Said Dr Walton. I could hear screams. When I saw it was Madame Dupont being attacked I had to do something. I have been looking after her teeth. Since she was a child.

Neighbour

He greets passersby in the street.

That tie doesn't match your shirt Sir !

Madam the vegetables you have bought are rotten !

It was your drinking Mate that caused your wife to leave !

A Country Life for Me

Herons on one leg in the pond Sir !
Rabbit & deer decorating edges of fields !
Ferns brushing my face at midnight !
A stately home on top of the hill
Pigsties at the bottom
Now
Where EXACTLY on the curve of the hill. Do I belong ?

Elastic Bands

As Fish Of The Day they nestle on the iced slab garlanded with
fresh parsley their pink and grey scales caught by falling
November light. Somewhat earlier Cardboard Pete climbed the
cobbled hill (ink and pen in his pocket) to ask for the hand of Emily
The Fishmonger's Daughter, whose manner of wrapping wet fish
in soft white paper, of stretching elastic bands over snapping crab
and lobster claws, brought him to his knees.

Launch

The worms enjoyed The History of Jam book launch immensely learning that jam existed thousands of years ago. That the banquets of The Sun King climaxed with spectacular confitures spread on gold leafed toasts proffered on bejewelled platters by scarlet robed wide eyed virgins. Did I say enjoy ? Why, they positively slithered to get their copy signed.

Vigil

It was because he stayed awake that there was night. Should he ever sleep. Night would end. To keep awake he wrote down everything. The times lights were turned. On and off. The number of dogs howling. Police sirens. Night trains. What people shouted in the street. Once. An eclipse. His head falling. On inked pages. At dawn.

Taivas

soft marshmallow sky
sky soft marshmallow
marshmallow sky soft
soft sky marshmallow
marshmallow soft sky
sky marshmallow soft

Descended

Please excuse my manners. It was only last Tuesday that I came down from the trees. On Wednesday I learnt how to make fire and walk upright. The following day to speak and write. On Friday I got a job starting Monday. Saturday I went shopping. Sunday got an early night. Today was my first day at work. May I buy you another drink ?

Below

A funnel in the ground provides him with air and light. Through this he is fed. Drink poured. Pages from his favourite books torn out. Poked down with a stick. One sentence at a time. If ever lonely. He shouts. Through the funnel. Demands he is sung too. By anyone. Anyone. Simply anyone. Anyone. Above.

Where Pearls Come From

A speck of dust in your head. Rolls round. Fattens itself. This is experienced as itching. Until smooth. Round. Translucent. Impossibly hard. You can of course wear it straight away. Ears and neck are close. Or place on velvet in a box. Swim with it. To the edge. Of the moon.

Marcel

When door designers lost their jobs. Door painters. Key cutters.
Hinge casters. Lost theirs. In the south coat hooks rusted on
shelves in boxes gathering dust. In the city Marcel the door
knocker maker rattled his handiwork gaining entrance to The
Unemployment Bureau.

Nature Watch

The badgers Smell love in your mouth. ███ How to
███ twist His eyes to seeing him. Next █ Champagne in the darkened room
Oysters. Candlelight rippling across silk sheets Speak. of cyclones,
pleasure. Marvellous. Breathes the cameraman. Bloody.
Marvellous.

Outline

Sl███████her m█████████████l. Draws round her in pencil. Adds mouth eyes nose. Draw█ delicate flowers in scribbled hair. Ad██████ speech bubble. Writes what she hears most often. We'll go away NEXT year. I PROMISE In her best ever. Joined up. Writing.

Flight Z45T7

From here things look tiny. A finger bigger than the Eiffel Tower.
Hand larger than a mountain. Meandering rivers shorter than the
hairs on my chest. Far below. A boy looks up. Draws a plane in
the sky. In his pocket diary. With a pencil stub.

Muddy Paws

The dogs cannot meet each other's eyes. Fools to heed talk of rich pickings buried beneath the hill now reduced to mounds of moist earth. Their panting breath laden with sighs they make good the holes they dug. Fur silvered by moonlight.

Dali Dad

The photograph reminded him how much his father resembled
Salvador Dali. Rolling his Rs. Twirling his moustache through the
streets of Croydon. Yelling down the hallway. Will someone
answer that bloody lobster !

Nightmare Supper

This glass is my house. Your red plate the field next door. The olive the monster out to get me. I bolt all the doors and windows. As it gets closer I realise I have forgotten the kitchen door. I hear the handle turning.[*]

[*] Young woman describes nightmare at supper.

Other People

The First enters the square with a sign that reads I AM LONELY !
The Second enters the corner opposite chanting LEAVE ME
ALONE ! They clash. A crowd gathers. They are arrested.
Found guilty.

Snowflake

We took the right fork and bought a Hemmer Stock Hybrid Squirrel Dog who I named Snowflake as snow fell the moment it leapt into the car. Sometimes I wonder. What would I have bought had I turned left.[*]

[*] Man tells how he got his dog.

Lost Property

With deft flicks. Soft strokes. Hand pats. She indicates the exact size and shape of her lost dog. Staff replicate her gestures to The Duty Manager who repeats their actions. Over the public address system.

Number 7 Deadly Sins, Arcacia Avenue, Tunbridge Wells

Walls burst with pride. Gluttons greedily consume grapes of wrath. Bills are paid slothfully. Carols sung lustfully. Grass green with envy.

Revenge

Back then. He was feted with flowers. Drinks served all round wherever he went. Now. Smirking faces chase him to the very edge of open land. Watch him dodge bolts of lightening.

Emergency

The box of red headed matches 56 in number made in Poland caught fire in Granddad's pyjama pocket which we filled with iced water from his bedside jug dousing the flames.

Newly Weds

At the reception they climb the cake. Tier after tier. Smear each other with fruit. With fresh cream. In-laws covering the bridesmaid's eyes. Best man. Speechless.

Well Worn

I like wearing a shirt just one more day. Crumpled. Tossed aside
the night before. Re-worn. Folds and creases resume my shape.
Collar and cuffs smudged soft grey.

Nativity Play

The lorry exits the theatre car park. Past Centurions on their mobiles. Wise Men smoking. Mary and Joseph kissing. Jesus gently winding up. The Donkey.

Newsagents Ad

Anyone who knows Ernie Mitchell please tell him to contact Brindi and Ellen. They need his muscles to move house. You can't miss him. He's got smashing eyes.

Waitress

Only once did she get an order wrong. A Tuesday. Seventh of September. 1954. He ran past the café. Naked. Table 6. One tea. Scrambled legs on toast.

Size Nines

Abandoned in the hallway. They plot revenge. Pinched flesh.
Heel blisters. You running along the shore. Water. Sand.
Between carefree toes.

Heaven v Hell

Hea⬛⬛⬛ trumpet⬛ ⬛raising T⬛ Lord. H⬛⬛uieter⬛⬛ ⬛ing. St⬛ Forbidden.

The Win█████

newborn █████ nurture ██████████████
█████ reaps ██████████████████ prize█

Super DIY Man

Plasters the ceiling standing on his head. Paints walls hands
behind back. Fixes taps whilst jogging. Sandpapers floors in his
sleep.

Ill Matched

They gaze at each other. She from the organic deli sipping freshly squeezed fruit juice. He from the market stall. Sauce bottle in hand.

Macaroon

She likes this word. More so when he says. I made them as a
child. Sweet cherry topped pyramids. A small kitchen. Stone cold
floor.

Drawers

They budge up. Rough and soft edges rubbing. Mutter to themselves. Another one tossed in. The very last thing we need.

H██o█t

Enter ███████████████████ the ████████
breath██ beneath ███████████████ him ████

These Things I Know

I ~~████████████████~~ No~~███████████████~~g Long Way ~~██~~ pera~~████████████~~ ff You. ~~█~~

Power

One person and one person only controlled school lunch menus during the 1970s. Their name . . . Mrs Sue Phillips.

Love

She nestles in his shirt pocket. An envelope of such delicate patterns. She washes. By hand. Come midnight.

New Name

Tried a new one yesterday. Connor. Connor is complex. More so than I. A simple soul. Wanting. A new name.

Seven Years Old

Saturday 25 June 1966. A mild day. Paperback Writer is number one in the charts. I walk the dog in the park.

■b ■ut

You ███████████████████████████ Sit. Wait █
███████████████████████ Listen.

Soles

Wea█████n more s███████████████████████████████ards.
Or from each other. Ever. E███████████████████

Masks

We made masks. Painted stripes. Spots. Fur. On balloon shapes. Varnished them. Swapped them.

Roast

Wreathed with spring greens broccoli onions carrots parsnips spuds. Embalmed with sage and onion.

Walls

Are fond of each other. Snuggle end to end. Herding space.
When they no longer give a damn. Fall.

Full Moon

Big. Fat. Stupid. Spoilt. Insistent. "Oh look at me ! look at me !"
It goes. Sucking light from the sun.

After Work

Chairs bang the tables. Windows whoop and holler. Drumroll
announces. The Paint Stripper !

Voyeur

An upstairs room. Possibly a kitchen. A dull light. A man. Or woman. Uses a back-scratcher.

Time

He maps all the stars he was the first to see. Names this new constellation. Sartagine.[*]

[*] Frying Pan

Made to Measure

Box lined with shredded suits. She calls her husband in. Lid.
Waiting to be nailed.

Love Match

Following the death of his mother and father he read their love match compatibility.

Listen . . .

They do not want you to know this. When no one is there. Doors
gather at windows.

Dog Drunk

Waking in trees. Nursing heads. What a night that was. Masters.
Leads. Nowhere !

Foie Gras

He stuffed love words down her throat. Her bloated heart never
stood a chance.

Car Tan

Countless roadworks. Layers of tarmac raising cars ever closer.
To the sun.

Road Trip

Crashing waves roll limbs. Beneath Ocean City Stars. Maryland Blue Eyes.

Evolution

The sea smoothes rocks into pebbles. Pebbles into sand. Sand into itches.

Banned

Carnivores gorge inside. Vegetarians huddle outside. Nibble in the rain.

ARE ! ARE NOT !

These ARE Henry Millers socks ! Those ARE NOT Henry Millers socks !

Evensong

Climbing the highest tree. Clears her throat. Duets with the clouds.

Flat Race

Saddled up. Under starter's orders. To the end of the hall and back.

Appointment

His excitement mounted as the day of his moustache fitting drew near.

Stick Up

They held the bank up with paper guns. Did time behind metal bars.

What He Would Have Wanted

After his funeral we went into his garden. Twirled. His umbrella.

For Sale

Plot. Good aspect. Between oak and elm. Would suit sapling.

Tower Block

The ceiling somebody's floor. The floor somebody's ceiling.

Compulsion

I, c, a, n, t, h, e, l, p, u, s, i, n, g, t, h, e, c, o, m, m, a,

Incognito

Where ever a country changed its name he moved there.

Born Idle

The brushes of the Sunday Painter. Monday to Saturday.

Eclipse

The child does not understand Do Not Look At The Sun !

Query

W h e; n d o; y; o u; u s; e t h; e s e; m; i c; o l o n;

Flat Out

In bed. Catching up with sleep. Some of it from 1976.

A Tree

Spreads its toes into the dark. Its arms into the light.

Favourite Words

Fromage. Pastoral. Tigerish. Battenberg. Lollop.

Period

I can't help. Using t. He. Fu. L. L. S. T. O. P.

Habit

I started smoking so I could hold my father's hand.

Lepus labium

You couldn't help but stare. The hare on her lip.

Last Night

I dreamt of sleepwalkers running in their sleep.

Christmas

A choir under the tree showered with needles.

Fact

Dogears help bookworms keep their place.

Ambition

He dreamt of being a peppered mackerel.

Lost Key

To open the door he removed its hinges.

Surgeon

Kickstarting the saw silences the birds.

Itch

Head Scratchers Of The World Unite !

Gale

The bird on the pole flaps in the wind.

Beauty v Boffin

She turns heads. He turns pages.

Play Time

Behind the tree peeks the school.

In bed

Wrapped In sheets of lightning.

Miracle

A flower in a field of stones.

Pathetic

A street light in sunshine.

I Must NOT

Touch The Chickens !

The Pigeon

Circles the square.